STRANMILLS COLLEGE BELFAST

SN 0074023 3

KV-196-085

THE

B·I·B·L·E WORLD

SETTLERS, WARRIORS AND KINGS
Champions of the Bible

Copyright © 1994 Lion Publishing

Text by John Drane

The author asserts the moral right
to be identified as the author of this work

Published by
Lion Publishing plc
Sandy Lane West, Oxford, England
ISBN 0 7459 2172 8
Albatross Books Pty Ltd
PO Box 320, Sutherland, NSW 2232, Australia
ISBN 0 7324 0542 4

First edition 1994

All rights reserved

Contributors to this volume
John Drane is Director of the Centre for the Study of Christianity
and Contemporary Society at the University of Stirling and the
author of several highly-acclaimed books on the Bible and its
background. In this book he presents the Bible and its history in a
way that young people can understand and enjoy.

Alan Millard, Rankin Professor of Hebrew and Ancient Semitic
Languages at Liverpool University, is the consultant for the
illustrations in this book, and all the books in the series.

Acknowledgments
All photographs are copyright © Lion Publishing, except the
following:
Alan Millard: 13;
Oxford Scientific Films: 10 (above left);
Rockefeller Museum, Jerusalem: 3 (below left).

The following Lion Publishing photographs appear by courtesy of:
the Amsterdam Bible Museum: 19 (above right);
the Trustees of the British Museum: 3 (top right);
the Eretz Israel Museum, Tel Aviv: 3 (below far left), 9, 10 (below
left);
the Museum of the History of Jersualem: 17;
the Temple Institute, Jerusalem: 19 (below right).

Illustrations, copyright © Lion Publishing, by:
Chris Molan: 1, 2, 3, 4, 5, 6, 7, 8 (right), 9, 10, 11, 14, 15 (right), 18,
20 (right)
Studio Simone Boni/Studio Luigi Galante: 8 (left), 12, 13, 15 (left),
16, 17, 19, 20 (left).

Maps and graphics, copyright © Lion Publishing, by:
Oxford Illustrators Ltd: 1, 2, 3, 4, 6, 9, 13, 14, 18.

Bible quotations are taken from the Good News Bible, copyright ©
American Bible Society, New York, 1966, 1971 and 4th edition
1976, published by the Bible Societies/HarperCollins, with
permission.

Story text is based on material from *The Lion Children's Bible*, by
Pat Alexander

A catalogue record for this book is available
from the British Library

Printed and bound in Malaysia

B·I·B·L·E W·O·R·L·D

SETTLERS, WARRIORS AND KINGS

CHAMPIONS OF THE BIBLE

John Drane

A LION BOOK

Contents

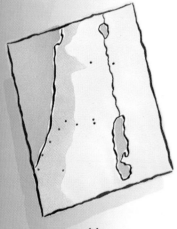

page 15

1 Out of Egypt

The great escape from Egypt was a turning point for the nation of Israel. In Egypt, the people had been slaves, making bricks for the king's huge building projects; but God chose a man named Moses to lead them to a land of their own.

It was a hard job. Some of the slaves were so poor and abused they didn't really want to escape. And the king of Egypt was certainly bent on keeping them. But Moses knew that God has a special concern for people who are poor and suffering, and he was determined to do as God wanted.

In the great escape from Egypt (the exodus), Moses had to fight many battles and face many enemies. But the people made it, across the sea and out into the desert that separated Egypt from the land they were heading for. With Moses as leader, people who had hardly known one another became close friends. Others joined them, attracted by the idea that a nation should be free to live their own lives in their own land.

Moses had a clear picture of the sort of nation God wanted these people to be. And he set them on the right path.

After the exodus from Egypt, Moses and the people of Israel spent forty years in the Sinai wilderness

▲ The Israelites who escaped from Egypt were a small nation and seemed unimportant in comparison with the powerful peoples that surrounded them. Yet God had a special plan for the Israelites and how they should live.

◀ Moses led the Israelite nation from slavery in Egypt to freedom: the freedom to live in ways that would please God.

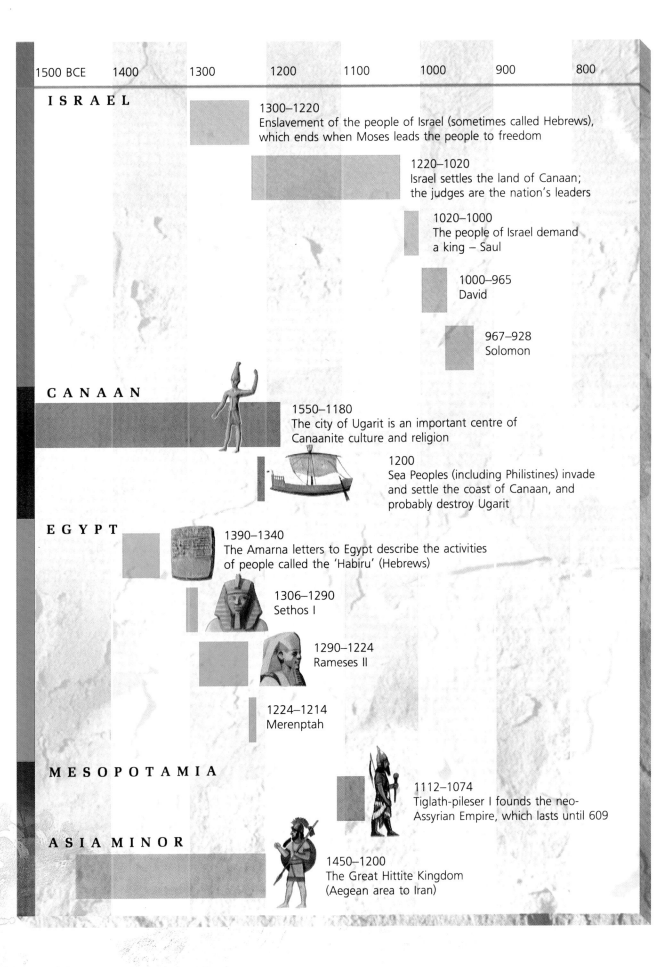

| 1500 BCE | 1400 | 1300 | 1200 | 1100 | 1000 | 900 | 800 |

ISRAEL

1300–1220
Enslavement of the people of Israel (sometimes called Hebrews), which ends when Moses leads the people to freedom

1220–1020
Israel settles the land of Canaan; the judges are the nation's leaders

1020–1000
The people of Israel demand a king – Saul

1000–965
David

967–928
Solomon

CANAAN

1550–1180
The city of Ugarit is an important centre of Canaanite culture and religion

1200
Sea Peoples (including Philistines) invade and settle the coast of Canaan, and probably destroy Ugarit

EGYPT

1390–1340
The Amarna letters to Egypt describe the activities of people called the 'Habiru' (Hebrews)

1306–1290
Sethos I

1290–1224
Rameses II

1224–1214
Merenptah

MESOPOTAMIA

1112–1074
Tiglath-pileser I founds the neo-Assyrian Empire, which lasts until 609

ASIA MINOR

1450–1200
The Great Hittite Kingdom (Aegean area to Iran)

2 The New Leader

Israel's first leader, Moses, was a great man. However, he was not the person who finally led the people of Israel into their new land. At the end of his life, in sight of the land of Canaan, he handed over to a new leader: Joshua.

Joshua was young, but he had special talents and skills. Before he became leader, Moses sent him to spy out the new land. His description of the figs and grapes and pomegranates that grew there made people's mouths water. There were people as big as giants in the land, but that did not worry Joshua: he knew that God would be with his people.

Joshua had learned that from Moses: he had caught Moses' vision of the sort of nation God wanted his people to be—a nation free to live their own lives in their own land. They would be free from slavery; free from cruelty and suffering; free to love God, and to live with other people in ways that would please God. They would share God's special concern for people who were poor and suffering.

Joshua was a good leader. He loved and trusted God, and he knew that with God's help ordinary people can do extraordinary things. He was someone others could trust and admire.

A fertile land

Canaan, home of the Canaanites, was a rich and prosperous country. It lay in the fertile crescent of land which curves from Babylonia in the east to Egypt in the west.

The Israelites were not the only people who wanted a share of its wealth. Other wandering tribes such as the Amalekites and the Midianites were keen to get their hands on it.

▼ When Joshua was sent to spy out the new land, he picked some of the summer fruit harvest to show the Israelites. But Joshua also saw some of the cruel and powerful people who ruled in Canaan.

Good advice for a new leader

God made this promise to Joshua:

'Be strong and courageous; don't be frightened or anxious. For I, the Lord your God, will be with you wherever you go.'

3 The Canaanites

Canaan—the land God had promised the Israelite people—was full of big cities. Each was a state in itself, ruled by its own strong king.

These Canaanite kings had no time for the new way of life that God had told Moses about and that Joshua wanted to turn into reality. In God's eyes, everyone is of equal value, and God's people were not to have favourites or take advantage of others who were weaker.

▶ **Canaanite rituals**
Rituals of Canaanite religion were carried out at shrines such as the one shown here, which is at Megiddo. Shrines were often built on hilltops and were called 'high places'.

▼ **Impressive finds**
The Canaanites had many skilled craftworkers. Remains of furniture and pottery dug up at Jericho indicate that they built comfortable homes for themselves, similar to the reconstruction shown here. The jewellery provides just a glimpse of some of the treasures they made for themselves and to sell to the international traders who were always moving through the land.

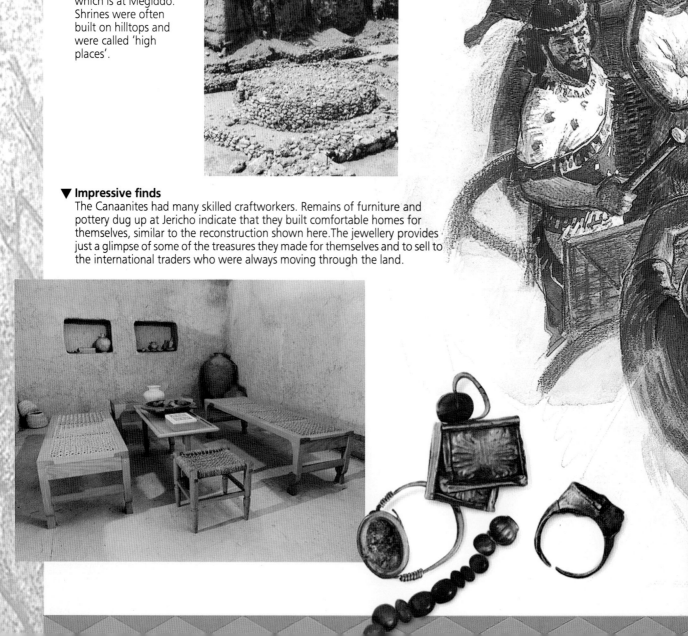

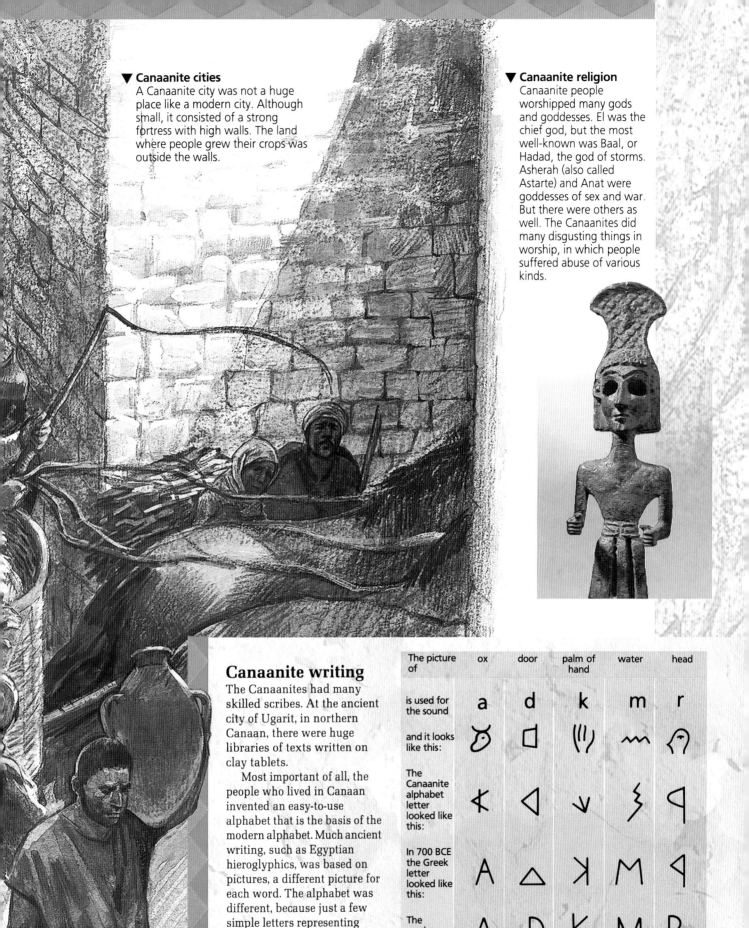

▼ Canaanite cities

A Canaanite city was not a huge place like a modern city. Although small, it consisted of a strong fortress with high walls. The land where people grew their crops was outside the walls.

▼ Canaanite religion

Canaanite people worshipped many gods and goddesses. El was the chief god, but the most well-known was Baal, or Hadad, the god of storms. Asherah (also called Astarte) and Anat were goddesses of sex and war. But there were others as well. The Canaanites did many disgusting things in worship, in which people suffered abuse of various kinds.

Canaanite writing

The Canaanites had many skilled scribes. At the ancient city of Ugarit, in northern Canaan, there were huge libraries of texts written on clay tablets.

Most important of all, the people who lived in Canaan invented an easy-to-use alphabet that is the basis of the modern alphabet. Much ancient writing, such as Egyptian hieroglyphics, was based on pictures, a different picture for each word. The alphabet was different, because just a few simple letters representing sounds could be used to spell out any word.

The picture of	ox	door	palm of hand	water	head
is used for the sound	a	d	k	m	r
and it looks like this:	𐤀	⸏	(ǁ)	∿	𐤓
The Canaanite alphabet letter looked like this:	𐤊	◁	⋁	⟑	𐤒
In 700 BCE the Greek letter looked like this:	A	△	K	M	⟑
The modern letter:	A	D	K	M	R

4 Towards Jericho

Joshua knew that not many Canaanite people would change their ways willingly, and so he made plans for battle in many cities. As part of the plan, he sent spies into the cities.

The spies discovered that some ordinary Canaanites liked Joshua's idea for a good society.

One of these was a woman named Rahab, who lived in a city called Jericho. She was a prostitute and knew what it felt like to be ill-treated by powerful men.

When Joshua's spies arrived, she made friends with them and helped them to escape capture. They promised that she and her family would live peacefully in the new Israelite state.

Joshua was encouraged by what the

▲ **City of palms**
Jericho is an oasis town built around precious springs of water. Its many palm trees make a bright splash of green in the surrounding desert.

spies told him. It would not be easy to overcome the armies of rich and powerful kings. But it would be worth the struggle, for the sake of people like Rahab who had already suffered enough, as well as for the slaves who had come from Egypt.

Rahab's descendants
Rahab was an ancestor of King David, Israel's greatest king, and the New Testament lists her as an ancestor of Jesus. Two other New Testament books describe her as a person of great faith. The people of Jericho looked down on her. But she was still important to God.

RAHAB'S BARGAIN

The Israelites were camped on the east bank of the Jordan. Their plan was to cross the river and capture the city of Jericho. Joshua sent two men to spy out the land and see if they could come up with a plan. The spies entered Jericho and found shelter at Rahab's house in the city walls. Rahab was a prostitute, abused by the Canaanite religion, and she was eager to learn more about the new kind of society the Israelites had to offer.

Meanwhile the king of Jericho had heard about the spies' arrival, and sent his men to deal with them. Where could Rahab hide the spies? Quickly she urged them to cover themselves under the drying flax laid out on the roof of her house, while she convinced the king's men that the spies had left.

Before the spies left that evening, Rahab asked a favour: that they spare her and her family when the Israelites took the city, in the same way that she had spared them.

'We owe you our lives,' replied the men, 'and we will not forget you, we promise.'

And Rahab let them down to safety out of her window in the city walls.

Across the river

The quickest way from Egypt to Canaan was along the coast. But as this map shows, Joshua and his people circled east. This way they could stay on the desert borders of the land and avoid meeting major enemies until they got well organized. But it also meant they had to cross the River Jordan before they could attack any of the big cities such as Jericho.

However, they knew God was with them, so remarkable things could happen. The very first thing was the River Jordan drying up to let them across in safety.

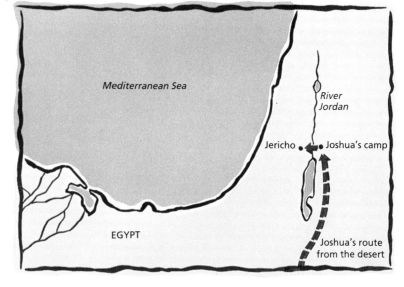

5 Jericho: The Astonishing Story

Jericho's position made it an important city for Joshua to capture. Unless he had, it would have been difficult for Israel to take control of the flat open plains just to the north. Joshua's military plan was to move up the centre of the country. That way, it would be easy for smaller groups of the people to settle peacefully in local areas.

▲ City walls
These ruined city walls from a later date give a good idea of what the walls might have looked like in Joshua's time.

◄ Springs of water
The springs of water at the Jericho oasis are still important today in supplying the town with water.

Did you know?

Jericho is the oldest city in the world. People lived there as long ago as 9000BCE. By the time Joshua arrived many cities had been built on the site at different times. The remains of previous cities were buried under the streets and houses of later ones.

Today, archaeologists can dig through the layers as if they were slicing a giant cake, and they can rediscover the history of a place in the rubble that has been left behind.

Almost nothing is left of the city of Jericho in Joshua's time. But at other cities such as Hazor, Lachish and Bethel, archaeologists have uncovered evidence of sieges and invasion from the time of Joshua.

THE FALL OF JERICHO

Fear swept through Jericho as the Israelites prepared to attack. The people barred the city gates and hid inside its massive walls.

Outside the city, Joshua thought of God's words: 'I have given you Jericho, its king and its army. Each day for six days you and your men must march round the city once. Seven priests bearing trumpets must lead the procession. On the seventh day, you and your men are to march round seven times, with the trumpets sounding. Then the priests must sound one long note while the men give a great shout, and the city walls will fall.'

Joshua and his men did just as God had said. When Joshua cried out, 'Shout! God has given you the city!' the walls came down and the Israelites took the city, destroying everything. Rahab and her family were spared, just as the spies had promised.

6 Making Friends and Defeating Enemies

The new way of life that Joshua brought with him was simple. As the people worshipped God, they remembered all that God had done in the life of their nation. Back in Egypt, God had shown great love for the oppressed slaves. If God was on the side of the poor, then God's people must be too.

Some Canaanites shared this vision of a new way of life, and welcomed the new arrivals to their land—people like the citizens of Shechem.

Joshua did not need to fight against their city, and Shechem soon became a great national centre.

Towards the end of his life, Joshua called a great national assembly to meet at Shechem. He invited others to make a solemn promise to serve God. The people knew they would be happier this way. 'We will serve the Lord,' they said.

Not everyone was glad to see the arrival of Israel in their new land. Israel's God demanded justice and fairness: equal shares for all. Kings would no longer be able to do as they liked with the lives and property of their subjects. They felt threatened.

Joshua often had to fight the strong armies of such tyrants—and win. Compared with the Canaanites, the Israelite people had quite primitive weapons. Canaan's kings had horses and chariots and their armies were able to cover long distances at great speed, while Joshua's soldiers had to move on foot. But the Israelites were brave people, and they believed in what they were fighting for.

Dividing the land

The book of Joshua contains many lists of people and places, showing which groups of people (families and tribes) got which pieces of land. Even great leaders like Joshua got the same amount as everyone else. His land was called Timnath-serah, meaning 'what is left'. Joshua was a generous man. He made sure others had a place to live first.

When he died, he was buried there at Timnath-serah, having done the work God called him for.

▼ This map shows how the land was divided among the tribes of Israel.

▲ **Shechem**
These are the ruins of the ancient city of Shechem, as they look today. In the time of Joshua, the Canaanites who lived at Shechem welcomed the Israelites and the new way of life they brought.

▼ **All in the family**
The whole family—young and old—were involved in building a new life for themselves in Canaan. Here, younger children mark the boundary of their land using stones picked from the area to be planted. Other family members plough and sow.

Settling the land

Land was very important to Joshua's people. Before, most of it had been owned by a few rich Canaanite kings. Under God's laws, all this had to change. Now, everything belonged to God—and God entrusted it to the care of the people. Everyone would have a share.

7 Judges

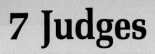

Joshua's successes in settling the new land were important. However, as most Canaanite cites were completely separate from one another, they had to be dealt with one by one. Other leaders continued the long process of winning the land after Joshua died.

The book of Judges tells that story. It is often a sad story—of how the Israelites forgot God and the kind of nation they should be and instead followed the old Canaanite ways. When they did this, they met with disaster. But when they turned back to the true God once more, the judges were able to help free them from their enemies.

These people called 'judges' did not work in law courts like judges today. They were called judges because they were concerned about justice. Sometimes they gave the people advice. When they saw something that was plainly wrong and unjust, they stepped in to put it right.

Just as God had seen what was wrong when the Israelites were slaves in Egypt and had acted to free them, so the judges were those women and men whom God called to rescue the people at particular times.

▲ **Battle site**
This picture is of Mount Tabor, the site of the battle between Sisera and the Israelites.

Deborah and Barak

Deborah and Barak were two famous judges, whose enemy was a man called Jabin. He was king of the city of Hazor and had a strong army, led by his cunning general, Sisera, to keep him in power. Sisera commanded 900 iron chariots and many thousands of fighting men.

Barak did not know whether he could ever beat such a powerful force. But Deborah knew that God wanted the Israelites to fight, and she encouraged Barak.

'This is the day on which the Lord has given Sisera into your hand,' she said. 'The Lord is going out before you in person'

Barak was still afraid to go alone, and Deborah had to offer to go with him. There was much hard fighting, but God was there—and Deborah and Barak won the victory.

Song of victory

The story of Deborah's victory is told in a long poem, written in a very old form of the Hebrew language. It tells how Barak needed different groups of Israelite tribes to join together and fight their common enemy. They fought Sisera's well-equipped chariots with only swords and spears. But eventually the battle was won when a sudden storm made the River Kishon overflow its banks. Sisera's iron chariots sank into the muddy ground.

Deborah's song

*'The kings came and fought;
the kings of Canaan fought,
but they took no silver away.
The stars fought from the sky;
as they moved across the sky,
they fought against Sisera.
A flood in the Kishon swept
them away...'*

8 Gideon

Canaanites were not the only enemies Israel's judges had to face. Gideon fought against a group of people called Midianites. They lived mostly in the desert, wandering around from one place to another. At harvest time the Midianites and other desert people called Amalekites regularly raided farms and houses. They had strong, fast camels, and no one could do much about them.

Gideon lived within easy reach of the desert, and greatly feared their raids. One night, he was threshing his own wheat in secret, so the Midianites would not find him, when an angel appeared.

The people had forgotten God, the angel said. They had even built an altar so they could worship the Canaanite god Baal. Gideon knew he had to destroy this altar.

So he did—in the middle of the night. But the angel also told him that he was the person God had chosen to free Israel. Gideon was not so sure about that. So he asked for proof . . .

Gideon asks for proof

Gideon laid a fleece outside overnight. He told God that he would believe the angel's message only if, the following morning, he found the fleece wet with dew and the ground dry. And that's how it was. The next night, he asked for the fleece to stay dry and the ground to be wet. When that happened, Gideon did as God wanted.

GIDEON'S ARMY

Gideon gathered a huge army to fight the Midianites. But God said to him, 'You have too many men. I don't want the Israelites to boast that they defeated the enemy in their own strength. No, I shall deliver Midian into your hands. Anyone who is frightened can go home now.' More than two thirds of the army went home and ten thousand were left.

God told Gideon there were still too many. God said, 'Take them down to the water to drink. I will tell you which ones to keep. Those who lap water out of their hands should stay, for they will not be taken by surprise. The ones who kneel down to drink must go home.' Gideon was left with only three hundred men.

In the middle of the night Gideon's men attacked the Midianite camp. They carried a trumpet in their right hands and a flaming torch, carefully hidden in an empty jar, in their left. Surprise and fear overcame the enemy as the trumpets blew. The jars were smashed and the torches blazed. All was confusion. The enemy ran away . . . and the battle was won.

Gideon's test

Gideon's test for good soldiers made sense. Those who knelt down to drink the water like a dog would be easily surprised by the enemy. But the three hundred who scooped up a drink in their hands could keep a close lookout all the time.

The Philistines

The Philistines were one of Israel's strongest enemies. They were not natives of the land of Canaan.

Ancient texts refer to the Philistines as part of the 'sea peoples'—nations who tried to invade Egypt, Canaan and Syria at about the time of Israel's escape from Egypt. They destroyed and captured cities in many countries, but they were not strong enough to defeat Egypt. In Canaan, they managed to find places to settle along the sea coast.

Powerful enemies

The Philistines became a strong and powerful nation in the land where the Israelites wanted to settle. But the Israelites could not accept the Philistine way of life unless they gave up doing what God wanted them to do.

Far from being concerned about fairness, the Philistine kings were real tyrants, and life must have been hard for ordinary people.

In the time of the judges, a man named Shamgar fought against the Philistines. So did Samson. But they were more powerful enemies than the Canaanites. It was only later, in the days of Saul and David, that the Philistines were finally defeated.

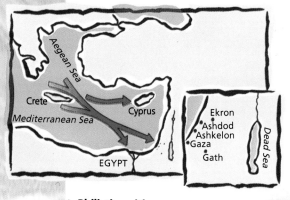

▲ **Philistine cities**
The Philistines who came across the sea to Canaan organized themselves into five city-states similar to those of the Canaanites. The cities were Gaza, Ashkelon, Ashdod, Ekron and Gath. Each of these cities had a tough king, who controlled everything and everybody.

◀ **Greek patterns**
The red and black geometric patterns on Philistine pottery are very similar to styles from the Greek islands at that time. The Philistines probably sailed across the sea to Canaan from these islands.

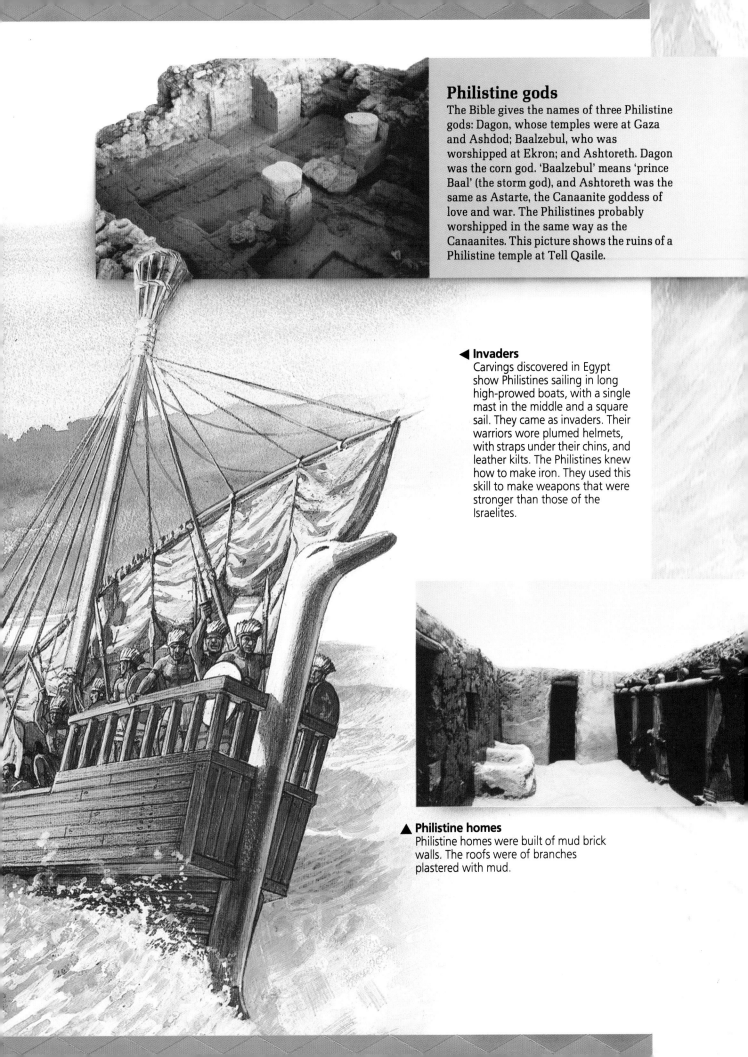

Philistine gods

The Bible gives the names of three Philistine gods: Dagon, whose temples were at Gaza and Ashdod; Baalzebul, who was worshipped at Ekron; and Ashtoreth. Dagon was the corn god. 'Baalzebul' means 'prince Baal' (the storm god), and Ashtoreth was the same as Astarte, the Canaanite goddess of love and war. The Philistines probably worshipped in the same way as the Canaanites. This picture shows the ruins of a Philistine temple at Tell Qasile.

◀ **Invaders**
Carvings discovered in Egypt show Philistines sailing in long high-prowed boats, with a single mast in the middle and a square sail. They came as invaders. Their warriors wore plumed helmets, with straps under their chins, and leather kilts. The Philistines knew how to make iron. They used this skill to make weapons that were stronger than those of the Israelites.

▲ **Philistine homes**
Philistine homes were built of mud brick walls. The roofs were of branches plastered with mud.

10 Samson the Strong

Samson, like Gideon, was one of the judges. He was to play a special part in freeing his people from their Philistine enemies.

From before he was born, Samson was special. For a long time his parents could not have children. Then one day God sent an angel to tell Samson's mother she was going to have a son. But she must drink no wine, and when the baby came, his hair must never be cut. He was to be dedicated to God as a 'Nazirite'. Samson was to be God's champion.

Samson had everything it takes to be a real hero. He was brave and amazingly strong. But he was disobedient to God, and it cost him his life.

Samson beats the Philistines

One day, as Samson was walking through the vineyards, a lion sprang out at him. Samson strangled the lion with his bare hands. Then he knew that God had given him special strength—and he began to use that strength against the Philistines.

Samson's Philistine enemies broke up his marriage. To get even, Samson tied burning torches to the tails of 300 foxes and released them in Philistine grain fields and olive orchards.

Samson used the jawbone of an ass to slay 1,000 Philistines who had come to capture and kill him.

When surrounded by Philistines, Samson escaped capture by ripping the gates out of a city wall.

The Philistines were enraged. They were out for his blood.

Nazirites

Samson was a Nazirite, specially dedicated to God. Nazirites promised never to cut their hair, drink wine, or touch a dead body. Other Nazirites mentioned in the Bible include Samuel and John the Baptist.

Did you know?

Samson's Philistine girlfriend, Delilah, tried to make Samson her prisoner by weaving his long hair into a loom. She may have used a vertical loom like this. The warp threads hung down from a beam and were held down with weights. The weaver would pass the weft threads—in Samson's case, hair—over and under the warp threads in turn. But Samson had no trouble breaking free.

SAMSON'S SECRET

What was the secret of Samson's strength? The Philistine rulers would have given anything to find out. So when Samson fell in love with a Philistine woman called Delilah, they seized their chance.

'Find out the secret of his strength,' they asked her. 'If we can get him, we'll give you eleven hundred silver coins.'

Delilah tried and tried to find out Samson's secret. Each time she asked, he gave a different answer. First she tied him up with seven bowstrings. That didn't work. Then she tied him up with new ropes; she even wove his hair into her loom. But he escaped every time. Eventually she wore him down with her questions.

'If you really love me,' she said, '*tell* me.'

'My hair has never been cut,' replied Samson. 'It is a sign that I was dedicated to God at my birth. If you cut my hair I'd be as weak as any other man.'

While Samson was asleep, Delilah sent for the Philistines. They cut his hair, and his strength was gone. His enemies tied him up; they blinded him and set him to work at a treadmill in the prison.

Months later, the rulers of the Philistines were worshipping their idol Dagon in their temple. They asked for Samson to be brought in so that they could mock him.

But time had passed. Samson's hair had grown, and he realized that all along it was God who gave him his strength, so he could help his people.

He silently prayed to God as he clung to the two great pillars of the temple. God restored his strength—he pushed on the pillars and the temple crashed down upon the Philistines. Samson died along with the enemies of his people.

11 Ruth

In contrast to all the stories of battles and warriors, the story of Ruth concerns one small family.

It begins with a man called Elimelech, who lived in the town of Bethlehem. At a time of famine he was forced to leave home and go to the country of Moab to look for food. He went with his wife, Naomi, and their two sons. They were Israelites, but in Moab both sons married local women.

The father and the sons died, and Naomi decided to go back home to Bethlehem. One of her daughters-in-law, Ruth, loved Naomi so much that she left her own people and went with her.

RUTH'S NEW FAMILY

Naomi was very poor, for widows had few rights and very little income. It was harvest time, so Ruth went into the fields each day to pick the leftover corn. In Israel, God's laws said that any corn not gathered by the harvesters could be freely taken by poor people.

One day Boaz, the owner of the field, noticed Ruth and asked who she was. He found out that she was the devoted daughter-in-law of his relative Naomi. Everybody had heard how this young foreign woman had left her own land and her own people to come to Israel with Naomi. Boaz called Ruth over and insisted she should gather corn from his fields, and offered her water to drink.

When Ruth told Naomi about Boaz that evening, Naomi was pleased. She secretly hoped that Boaz would marry Ruth, for God's law said that when a woman was widowed the husband's nearest male relative should provide for her by marrying her. Boaz admired the loving way that Ruth, a stranger in a foreign land, cared for her aged mother-in-law. Within a short time Boaz did ask Ruth to marry him. So, God took care of this woman from a foreign land. Ruth and Boaz were married, and their son became the grandfather of Israel's great king, David.

Caring for the poor

God's laws always had a special place for poor people. The reapers left some corn behind in the fields so that poor people could do as Ruth did—go and gather some for themselves. God's law said:

> 'When you harvest your fields, do not cut the corn at the edges of the fields . . . leave them for poor people and foreigners.'

This was very different from the Canaanite way of life. The Israelites always tried to remember that they had been slaves in Egypt. Everything they had came through God's love and generosity.

Because God is loving and generous, God's people should live that way too. It was often easier to live like the Canaanites. But the story of Ruth reminded them of God's true standards.

12 Samuel: Last of the Judges

Samuel is sometimes called 'the last of the judges'.

He had been a special person right from the beginning. Long before he was born, his mother Hannah had prayed to God for a child. In the ancient world, every grown-up wanted to have children. They saw babies as a special sign of God's blessing, and they also needed children to help with work and to look after them in their old age. Hannah had to wait a long, long time... but eventually she did have a son. She was so grateful to God that she brought him up as a Nazirite (like Samson). And when Samuel was still a child he went to live at the temple at Shiloh.

It must have been hard for him to be all alone there with just the old priest Eli for company. His parents only visited once a year. But God did not forget him.

▼ **The temple at Shiloh**
The Bible says that the tent of meeting—God's special tent—was set up at Shiloh when the Israelites first settled in Canaan. By the time of Eli a temple had been built to replace the tent. This photo shows the ruins of ancient buildings that have been discovered at Shiloh.

▼ Because of its temple, Shiloh became an important religious centre. Once a year, people used to come from miles away for the festivals that marked the end of harvest.

THE BOY IN THE TEMPLE

Each night the boy Samuel slept in the temple. The old priest, Eli, slept there too. One night Samuel woke up suddenly.

'Samuel!' said a voice.

'Here I am!' he replied and ran to Eli. But Eli had not called him.

'Go back to bed,' he said.

Then it happened a second time.

And a third. By now Eli realized that it was God who was calling, and told Samuel what to do when he heard the voice again. So when Samuel heard the voice again he said, 'Speak, for your servant is listening.'

And God spoke.

God's message to Samuel

God's message was that Eli's sons would be punished because they had said evil things about God. Samuel would be the prophet who would lead the people of Israel.

All this came true. As a grown man, Samuel told the people to stop worshipping the gods of other nations, such as Baal and Ashtoreth, and live by God's laws.

When they did so, they beat their old enemies, the Philistines, and the nation was at peace. Samuel helped the people to feel they were all part of the same nation, even though they came from different tribes. Every year, Samuel would travel round to different places giving the people advice and helping them to settle their disagreements.

▲ Samuel was only a young boy when God spoke to him so suddenly. Most people would have expected God only to speak with Eli and his sons, the full-time priests in charge of the temple in Shiloh. But God can use very ordinary people. Many centuries later, Jesus said that children would have a special place in God's kingdom.

13 Saul: The First King

Israel's last judge, Samuel, was growing older. The Philistine armies seemed to get stronger every day—and the leaders of the Israelite tribes were at their wits' end. They went to the temple at Shiloh, took God's covenant box—the ark—and carried it into battle with them. They thought that if the enemy saw that, they would run away.

But it didn't work. Instead, the Philistines captured the covenant box itself, and defeated Israel yet again.

Their success was short lived. Plague broke out in the cities where the Philistines took the ark. In the end they hitched it to a team of oxen and sent it back to the Israelites.

For many years, all was well. But as Samuel grew older, the Israelites began to worry: who would be their leader when he died?

'Surely,' they said to Samuel, 'we need a king.'

But Samuel was not sure this was the right answer. From the very start, God had been their king. The slaves who escaped from Egypt had lived by following God's laws.

When enemies threatened them God had always given them courageous leaders to deliver them. So why did they need a king who would have power all the time? Samuel gave the people a serious warning about what would happen.

Samuel's warning

'This is what your king will do to you,' Samuel said. 'He will make your sons soldiers in his army. You will have to farm the land for him, and make his weapons. He will take your best cattle and crops and land. And you will become his slaves. That is what kings are like. You will be sorry you ever asked for a king.'

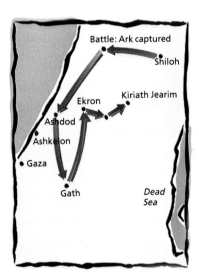

Journeys of the ark
The Philistines captured the Israelite ark in battle and took it to the city of Ashdod. But disaster struck, so they sent the ark to Gath. The same thing happened. When disaster struck a third time at Ekron, they decided to send the ark back to the Israelites.

Map labels:
Battle: Ark captured
Shiloh
Kiriath Jearim
Ekron
Ashdod
Ashkelon
Gaza
Gath
Dead Sea

The warning ignored

Samuel's warning rang true for some. They remembered the cruelty of the Canaanite kings. But in the end the majority of the people decided they would have their own king. Samuel went along with them.

It didn't take them long to find one. Saul belonged to the little tribe of Benjamin; but he was a brave warrior, and he stood head and shoulders above everyone else—literally! It was obvious that he was the right person.

Anointing

When Samuel realized that Saul was to be the first king of Israel, he anointed him by pouring oil on his head. At that time priests were anointed like this—and so was some of the furniture used in worship at the various temples. It meant that the person or the object was appointed to serve God in a special way. Saul was not only to be a military leader: he would also be God's special representative.

▲ Samuel may have used a little jug like this when he anointed Saul.

◀ **Reluctant hero**
Although Samuel had anointed him, Saul panicked when the day came for declaring who would be king. At a great assembly of the people of Israel, Saul's family had to drag him from his hiding-place among the baggage so that Samuel could introduce him to the people.

14 Saul: A Bold Leader

Saul turned out to be a good leader. He was exactly what the people wanted: bold, courageous—and always listening to God. His skill as a soldier was put to the test not long after he became king.

The town of Jabesh-gilead was a fair distance from most other Israelite cities—away on the opposite side of the River Jordan. It was an easy place for enemies to attack, especially enemies like the Ammonites, who lived on the fringes of the desert.

One morning, the people of Jabesh-gilead woke up to find their town surrounded by an enemy army. There was little they could do, because help was so far away and would take some time to arrive. So they tried to strike a bargain with the enemy. They offered to become the subjects of the Ammonites. But the enemy leader was a cruel and harsh man. He insisted

that as part of the bargain he should be allowed to put out everyone's right eye.

There was no way the people of Jabesh-gilead would allow that. Not without a fight, anyhow. They secretly sent a messenger to Saul on the other side of the river. When Saul heard what was happening, he got together a large army and made the long journey to fight the Ammonites. It was a fierce battle, but Saul won.

There was no doubt left in anyone's mind that Saul was a good king! Not long after this, his coronation was celebrated in grand style at

▼ **King without a kingdom**
Saul was never fully in control of his kingdom. In the south, there were still three powerful Canaanite cites: Jerusalem, Aijalon and Gezer. In the north, the Philistines controlled all the important roads. Saul stayed in his own fortress at Gibeah, and the people began to feel they hardly knew him.

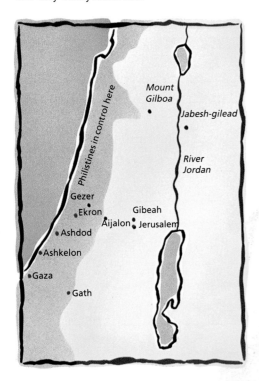

Philistines in control here

Mount Gilboa
Jabesh-gilead
River Jordan
Gezer
Ekron
Gibeah
Aijalon Jerusalem
Ashdod
Ashkelon
Gaza
Gath

Gilgal, another of the great religious centres of the land. Saul had made a great start to his reign. But before long, he began to do some of the unpleasant things Samuel had warned about. Instead of just gathering an army whenever an enemy appeared, Saul set up his own full-time army to serve and protect himself. And since he was not a rich man, he made his people pay for it all in taxes.

▼ **Saul's harsh rule**
Saul's private army cost a great deal to train and to keep ready for action. Even the poor had to pay taxes to support it. Saul soon became very unpopular.

15 David: Shepherd and Giant-Killer

As time passed by, Saul became more and more unpopular with his people. If his army had been strong enough to defeat the strong Philistine enemies, that would have been all right. But Saul and his soldiers made no progress at all. As a result, Saul became very depressed and moody. He felt he could no longer trust people, not even Samuel. He refused to accept advice from others and became lonely and withdrawn.

The arrival of David on the scene did nothing to make Saul feel more confident. David came from a humble family and worked as a shepherd. He also had an exceptional talent for playing the harp and was brought to Saul's household in the hope that he could soothe the king with his music.

But within a short time David shot to fame as the hero who defeated the Philistines.

◀ When he fought Goliath, David chose five rounded pebbles as ammunition for his slingshot. They would have been about this size.

Slingshot hotshot

When David went to kill Goliath he took with him just five smooth stones and his slingshot. This was a simple weapon that every child in Israel played with, and also a weapon of war. David would have used the slingshot to scare off wild animals that threatened his sheep.

GOD'S CHAMPION

The Israelite army faced the Philistines across the Valley of Elah. The Israelites were terrified—this was a strange war. For each morning Goliath marched out of the Philistine camp shouting taunts at the Israelites.

Goliath was no ordinary soldier. He was huge—about three metres tall; he wore a bronze suit of armour and carried a spear as thick as a bar on a weaver's loom.

'You coward Israelites!' shouted Goliath. 'If one of you comes out and kills me, we'll surrender. But if I kill him...' He laughed grimly.

None of the Israelites dared face Goliath... until David arrived. David was only a shepherd boy. He had been sent

by his father with provisions for his three elder brothers who were in the army.

When David heard Goliath's sneers, he was furious. 'How dare this Philistine insult God's people?' he said. 'Take me to Saul—I'll fight Goliath.'

The soldiers laughed and Saul was doubtful. 'You're only a boy,' he said.

'I may be only a boy,' replied David, 'but when I'm looking after my father's sheep I have to protect them. I have rescued sheep from lions and bears and God has looked after me—and he will now too.'

Eventually Saul was convinced. 'May God be with you,' he said, and he offered David his own armour to wear. But David took just his shepherd's stick and chose five smooth stones from the stream. His sling was in his hand, ready. David approached Goliath.

Goliath laughed. 'A boy! The champion of Israel?' he roared.

David replied, 'You have a sword, a spear and a javelin, but I come to you in the name of the God of Israel, whom you mock. This God will give you and all the Philistines into my hands.'

Immediately David took out a stone and loaded his sling. He whirled the sling, and threw. The stone hit Goliath on the forehead and he fell down senseless. Then, seizing Goliath's own sword, David cut off the giant's head.

When the Philistines saw what had happened they turned and ran, with the Israelites following. And so the battle was won.

16 David: Warrior and Poet

David's victory over Goliath made him Israel's new hero. He was the special friend of Jonathan, Saul's eldest son. But he was not popular with Saul, who became very jealous of David. Saul hunted him down with his armies and David was forced to live like an outlaw, hiding in remote places with only his own friends for support.

Popular hero

David's success at dodging Saul's soldiers made him even more of a popular hero.

More and more, people began to see him as the obvious person to be the next king. David was already well aware that this was his future: years before, Samuel had seen him as God's choice, and had secretly anointed him.

But David did not try to seize power: he knew that God would choose the right time for him to become king.

▲ The picture above shows the stream below David's waterfall, flowing between rocky crags.

Saul defeated

Saul continued to wage a desperate war against the Philistines. In the end he died in a fierce battle with them on Mount Gilboa. When he realized he was going to lose, he killed himself, rather than live to be tortured by the Philistines. His sons died with him—including Jonathan, whom David loved as his dearest friend.

David mourned their death:

'Saul and Jonathan, beloved and lovely! In life and in death they were not divided. How are the mighty fallen in the midst of battle.'

◀ **David's waterfall**
This cascading stream at En Gedi brings green growth in the barren Judean desert. The place, with its water and its caves, has long been associated with David. It would have made an excellent hide-out and would have been a good source of water for an outlaw such as David. It is known as David's waterfall.

David the poet

David had a deep love for God. He used his talent for composing songs to share his deepest feelings about God with other people.

Jewish tradition says that David wrote the psalms of the Old Testament—a collection of wonderful poems on many different religious themes, such as love for God, trust in God, prayers for help and songs of praise. David did not write them all, but he certainly worked on some of them. They all show a great devotion to God and a determination to live by God's laws.

▲ David's harp
This picture shows David playing a type of harp called a *kinnor*. As a boy, he probably had only a homemade instrument—perhaps a piece of forked branch with strings tied from one side to the other.

The psalms

The psalms were used as a hymn book by many generations of Jewish worshippers. They were often sung on grand occasions, with a complete orchestra providing the music. Some psalms had movement and dance to go along with them. They were sung in special ceremonies that covered every season of the year.

Psalm 23

The Lord is my shepherd;
I have everything I need.
He lets me rest in fields of green grass
and leads me to quiet pools of fresh water.
He gives me new strength.
He guides me in the right paths,
as he has promised.
Even if I go through the deepest darkness,
I will not be afraid, Lord,
for you are with me.
Your shepherd's rod and staff protect me.

You prepare a banquet for me,
where all my enemies can see me;
you welcome me as an honoured guest
and fill my cup to the brim.
I know that your goodness and love will be with me
all my life;
and your house will be my home as long as I live.

17 David: A Great King

Soon after Saul died, David became king. But he had to deal with the many disagreements between different groups that had developed during Saul's reign. David's first job was to try to bring them all together. They needed a complete break from the past, and David gave it to them by setting up a new capital city: Jerusalem.

Jerusalem was called 'David's city' because David himself captured it from the Canaanites (who called it Jebus) with a small group of his élite troops. With a new king and a new capital city, the nation began a new period of security and prosperity.

Jerusalem

Jerusalem was an impressive city to begin with. David set out to make it even bigger and better. He brought in skilled workers from other countries, and they designed and built a new palace that would be as grand as the palaces other kings had.

David also defeated all Israel's traditional enemies, including the dreaded Philistines. For the very first time, Israel was in control of most of the land.

In all of this, David never forgot his people's history. They had been slaves in Egypt, and it was only God's love that had rescued them. The covenant, that was kept in the ancient covenant box (the ark), was the sign of that—and David arranged for it to be brought into Jerusalem in a special ceremony. From now on, Jerusalem was not only the capital city of David's nation. It was the most special place for God to be worshipped.

▼ **In the tunnel**
David's soldiers would have had to crawl through some parts of the water tunnel into the city.

A cunning plan
David captured the Canaanite city he renamed Jerusalem by cunning. He and his men found a way into a tunnel that led from an underground spring of water outside the city to a water shaft inside the walls.

An imperfect king

David was a great king, but his home life was far less successful. He arranged to have Uriah, one of his finest generals, killed so he could marry Uriah's wife, the lovely Bathsheba. The prophet Nathan told him clearly that this did not please God.

Later, David's own favourite son, Absalom, led a rebellion against him. There was civil war, and Absalom died in a great battle against David's army. David was broken-hearted.

A special promise

God made a special promise to David:

'You will always have descendants, and I will make your kingdom last forever.'

Jesus was one of David's descendants, and Christians believe that his kingdom will last for all time.

▼ David's city

This model shows how the city of Jerusalem may have looked in David's time. Low, mudbrick buildings are huddled together inside the city walls, but there are a few larger buildings for the king and his household.

18 Solomon

Solomon was the next king after David. He became king because he was David's son, as God had promised David.

Solomon was a tough king. He built up a big army, with thousands of chariots and horses. There was no doubt now who was in control of the whole land of Israel. Solomon's kingdom was the strongest for miles around. He had his own empire, and even took taxes from other nations. As a result, he grew rich and famous.

He never needed to be a great warrior himself. Saul and David had fought all the battles, and Solomon had few enemies. In fact, he made all sorts of agreements with other nations.

A time of prosperity

Most of the other kingdoms were more advanced than Israel. Solomon built fleets of ships and set up new industries, using the precious materials he could buy from other lands. When Solomon decided to build magnificent new buildings in Jerusalem, he sent for the finest craft workers from Tyre to come and design them.

▼ **International trade**
This map shows the chief trade routes through Israel in Solomon's day.

Horses from Cilicia

Damascus

to MESOPOTAMIA

Tyre

King Hiram of Tyre sent ships loaded with cedar wood for Solomon's Temple.

Joppa

Jerusalem

Horses and chariots from EGYPT

Ezion-geber

From Arabia, including the land of the Queen of Sheba, came spices, gold and precious stones

From East Africa came ships laden with wood, precious stones, silver, ivory and gold.

▲ Copper mines
These tunnels in the rock face near
Ezion-geber are the openings of shafts
to copper mines that were used in King
Solomon's day.

◀ Trading ships
This scene of the harbour at Ezion-geber
shows precious cargo being unloaded
from Solomon's fleet of trading ships.
King Hiram of Tyre (the Phoenician city
famous for its merchant trading) sent
seamen to work with Solomon's men.

Solomon and his wives

One way of showing
friendship to other nations
was for the king to marry a
wife from each of them. As a
result, Solomon had many
wives of different races. Some
people in Israel were not
pleased with this, as the
foreign wives naturally
wanted to bring their own
gods and customs with them.

19 Solomon Builds a Temple

David had brought God's covenant box into the city of Jerusalem. It was very precious to the people of Israel: when the people saw it, they remembered God's love for their ancestors who had been slaves in Egypt. It reminded them of God's laws for them to follow. And they wanted to give it pride of place in their new capital.

Long before Solomon became king, David had chosen the site for a grand temple where the covenant box would be kept safe. But Solomon built it. He bought all the finest materials and employed the best builders—no expense spared. The Israelite people were tough soldiers, but they had less experience in designing beautiful buildings, so Solomon asked other nations for advice. He got a lot of help from Hiram, the king of Tyre, who supplied special wood, as well as many of the workers.

The work took seven years. But when it was finished, it was a building the whole nation could be proud of. In a grand ceremony, the special covenant box was carried into the innermost room of the temple (God's special place), and there was a great celebration. From now on, people would always come to Solomon's temple for the big religious festivals of the year.

Solomon became famous because of his temple. Hundreds of year later, people remembered him for it.

Who pays?

Solomon was not always popular with his own subjects. Most of the ordinary people lived in small villages scattered around the countryside. They had to pay heavy taxes, which Solomon spent on the temple and on luxurious palaces for himself and his many wives.

◀ Treasures great and small
At the entrance to the temple stood two huge free-standing pillars, called Jachin and Boaz.
Intricately decorated vessels were crafted from pure gold for use within the temple.
The modern reproductions shown here give a hint of what the real objects might have been like.

Inside the temple

Everything for the temple had to be made by hand. Precious metals had to be cast, wood had to be carved, stone had to be cut to size, beautiful embroideries had to be worked. And then it all had to be put together.

This picture shows the cedar-panelled walls that have been carved and overlaid with gold. Squares of beaten gold are being laid over the wooden floor. Beyond is the Holy of holies, where two olive-wood cherubim covered with gold symbolize God's protection of the covenant box.

The artist has shown the doors to the Holy of holies, to let us see inside at the point when building work was nearly complete. Once the building was finished, no one went into the Holy of holies except the High Priest, just once a year, on the Day of Atonement.

Solomon's prayer

When the temple was finished, Solomon stood in front of the altar and said a prayer:

'*Lord God of Israel, there is no god like you in heaven above or on earth below. You keep your covenant with your people and show them your love when they live in whole-hearted obedience to you. You have kept the promise you made to my father David ... But can you, O God, really live on earth? Not even all heaven is large enough to hold you, so how can this temple that I have built be large enough? ... Hear my prayers and the prayers of your people when they face this place and pray. Hear us in your home in heaven and forgive us.*'

20 Solomon's Wisdom

God had promised to make Solomon wise—and Solomon got quite a reputation as a wise man. The Bible says he composed 3,000 proverbs, and became an expert in all sorts of subjects from the study of the stars to the study of animals and the natural world.

Because Israel was at peace under his rule, there was plenty of time and opportunity for people to set up schools, to write books, and to explore the world around them.

Writing the Bible

History writers began to write down the long story of how a ragged crowd of slaves had become a great nation. During Solomon's time, the stories of Moses, Joshua, and other great leaders were first written down.

Temple music

Now that there was a temple, the people needed new songs to be used in the worship of God. The first song books were put together. Musicians found work in the temple orchestra. Actors and dancers were needed as well—for worship was a great spectacle.

Here are some of the Bible's proverbs:

'The Lord wants weights and measures to be honest and every sale to be fair.'

'Without wood, a fire goes out; without gossip, quarrelling stops.'

'Lazy people should go and watch ants at work—and take a lesson from them! People who don't bother to work will end up poor.'

Solomon's writing

Jewish tradition says that Solomon himself wrote some Bible books—Proverbs, Ecclesiastes, and the Song of Solomon.

Ecclesiastes is quite a miserable book: whoever wrote it asked a lot of questions about what the point of being alive was, but decided in the end that people should enjoy life while they could.

The song of Solomon is a collection of poems between a woman and her lover.

Proverbs contains wise sayings about all kinds of subjects.

THE QUEEN OF SHEBA

King Solomon was wise and he was wealthy. His fame, and the news of the magnificent temple he had built in Jerusalem, spread far and wide.

Away across the desert, the Queen of Sheba, famed for her great riches, decided to go and see for herself if what was said about Solomon's wisdom was true. She would test him with hard questions. Was he really as wealthy as people said? She took rich gifts: a caravan of camels laden with spices, large quantities of gold and precious stones.

And what about the temple? She would have to see it to believe it.

Solomon answered all her questions easily. He showed her his riches and took her to visit the temple. The Queen of Sheba was dazzled by it all.

'Now I have seen it with my own eyes,' she said. 'You are far wiser and richer than I thought. Your God has blessed you. Your people have a king who is just and fair.'

She gave Solomon the gold, the spices and the jewels she had brought with her, and King Solomon gave her gifts in exchange. Then the Queen set out on the long journey home.

Finding Out More

If you want to know more about what you have read in *Settlers, Warriors and Kings*, you can look up the stories in the Bible.

There is a standard way to refer to Bible passages, and it is used here. Each Bible book is split into chapters and verses. Take **1 Samuel 9:1–27**, for example. This refers to the first book of Samuel (there are two of them); chapter number 9: verses 1–27.

1 Out of Egypt

Israel

Exodus chapters 1–12
Exodus chapters 12–40
Joshua
Judges
1 Samuel
2 Samuel
1 Kings chapters 1–2
1 Kings chapters 2–11

Mesopotamia

2 Kings 15:19
1 Chronicles 5:26
Joshua 1:4

2 The New Leader

Deuteronomy 31:1–8; 34:9; Joshua as Moses' successor
Joshua chapters 1–3

Judges chapters 6–8
Exodus 17:8–15
Joshua 1:9

3 The Canaanites

Joshua 11:1–5	Canaanite kings
Leviticus 19:14–15	Laws of justice
Numbers 34:50–52	Destroying the idols
1 Kings 18:16–40	Elijah and the prophets of Baal

4 Towards Jericho

Hebrews 11:31; James 2:25	Rahab in the New Testament
Joshua 2:1–21	Joshua and the spies in Jericho
Joshua chapter 3	The Israelites cross the Jordan

5 Jericho: The Astonishing Story

Joshua chapter 6	The fall of Jericho

6 Making Friends and Defeating Enemies

Joshua chapter 24	Joshua speaks to the people at Shechem
Joshua chapter 10	The Amorites are defeated
Joshua chapters 13–21	Dividing the land
Joshua 24:29–30	Joshua is buried

7 Judges

Judges 2:11–23	The people of Israel forget God
Judges 4:4–10	Deborah and Barak
Judges chapter 5	The song of Deborah and Barak
Judges 5:19–21	

8 Gideon

Judges chapter 6	Gideon
Judges 6:36–40	Gideon and the fleece
Judges 7:1–21	Gideon defeats the Midianites

9 The Philistines

1 Samuel 5:1–5	Dagon
Judges 2:11–13	Ashtoreth
2 Kings 1:16–17	Baalzebub

10 Samson the Strong

Judges chapter 13	Samson's birth
Judges 14:5–6; 15:1–5, 16–17; 16:2–3	Samson beats the Philistines
Judges 12:7; 1 Samuel 1:11; Luke 1:15	Nazirites
Judges 16:4–22	Samson and Delilah
Judges 16:23–30	Samson's death

11 Ruth

Ruth 1:1–18	Naomi and Ruth return to Bethlehem
Ruth chapters 2–4	Ruth and Boaz
Leviticus 19:9–10	Law about harvest
Deuteronomy 25:5–6	Law about widows
Exodus 22:22–27	Laws to help the poor
Leviticus 19:9–10	

12 Samuel: Last of the Judges

1 Samuel 1:1–18	Hannah prays for a child
Psalm 127:3–5	Children are a sign of God's blessing
Joshua 18:1	The temple at Shiloh
1 Samuel chapter 3	Samuel in the temple
1 Samuel 7:3–17	Samuel builds up the nation

13 Saul: The First King

1 Samuel chapters 4–6	Travels of the covenant box
1 Samuel chapter 9	The lost donkeys
1 Samuel 8:11–18	Warning about a king
1 Samuel 10:1	Samuel anoints Saul
1 Samuel 10:22–23	Saul hides

14 Saul: A Bold Leader

1 Samuel chapter 11	Saul defeats the Ammonites

15 David: Shepherd and Giant-Killer

1 Samuel 16:14–16	Saul is depressed
1 Samuel 17:20–54	David and Goliath

16 David: Warrior and Poet

1 Samuel 19–26	David and Saul
1 Samuel 16:13	Samuel anoints David secretly
2 Samuel 1:23, 27	

17 David: A Great King

2 Samuel 5:6–7	David attacks Jerusalem
2 Samuel 5:9–12	David builds his city
2 Samuel chapters 11–12	David and Bathsheba
2 Samuel chapters 15–18	David and Absalom
2 Samuel 7:16	

18 Solomon

1 Kings 4:21	Solomon's kingdom
1 Kings chapter 5	Solomon prepares to build the temple
1 Kings 11:1–4	Solomon and his wives

19 Solomon Builds a Temple

1 Kings chapters 6–8	Solomon builds the temple

20 Solomon's Wisdom

1 Kings 4:29–34	Solomon the wise man
1 Kings 10:1–13	The Queen of Sheba's visit
Proverbs 16:11	
Proverbs 26:20	
Proverbs 6:6–11	

Index